Diving Boards
&
Trampolines

Vol. I

DIVING BOARDS & TRAMPOLINES
Vol. I

88 MEDITATIONS TO LAUNCH YOU
INTO PURPOSEFUL LIVING

AMY LAYNE LITZELMAN
www.AmyLayneLitzelman.com

Window of Worship Publishing

Diving Boards and Trampolines Vol. I
Copyright © 2015 Amy Layne Litzelman. All rights reserved.

No part of this publication may be reproduced, stored in a retrieval system or transmitted in any way by any means, electronic, mechanical, photocopy, recording or otherwise without the prior permission of the author except as provided by USA copyright law.

Scripture quotations marked (AMP) are taken from the Amplified Bible, Copyright © 1954, 1958, 1962, 1964, 1965, 1987 by The Lockman Foundation. Used by permission.

Scripture quotations marked (NIV) are taken from the Holy Bible, New International Version®. niv®. Copyright© 1973, 1978, 1984 by International Bible Society. Used by permission of Zondervan. All rights reserved.

Scripture quotations marked (NKJV) are taken from the New King James Version®. Copyright © 1982 by Thomas Nelson, Inc. Used by permission. All rights reserved.

Scripture quotations marked (NLT) are taken from the Holy Bible, New Living Translation, copyright © 1996. Used by permission of Tyndale House Publishers, Inc., Wheaton, Illinois 60189. All rights reserved.

Scripture quotations marked (ESV) are from The Holy Bible, English Standard Version®, copyright © 2001 by Crossway Bibles, a publishing ministry of Good News Publishers. Used by permission. All rights reserved.

Scripture quotations marked (NASB) are from The Holy Bible, New American Standard Version®, copyright © 1995 by Lockman Foundation. Used by permission. All rights reserved.

Published in the United States of America
ISBN: 978-0-9965098-2-4
1. Religion, Christian Life, Devotional
2. Religion, Christian Life, Spiritual Growth

"As he was speaking, a woman in the crowd called out,
'God bless your mother –
the womb from which you came,
and the breasts that nursed you!'

Jesus replied,
*'But even more blessed are all who hear the word of God
and put it into practice.'"*

Luke 11:27-28, NLT (emphasis mine)

Introduction

During my college years I traveled with a group of friends to a lake house for the weekend. My friend's family owned a boat and they all loved to waterski. I, on the other hand, knew nothing about the sport. It came my turn to try and my heart swelled in my chest. I so longed to jump up and give it a go, but logic and fear rushed up to remind me, *"You don't even know how to swim! How are you going to feel when you make a fool of yourself?"*

I was wearing a life vest, my friends were willing to teach me, they were even cheering me on, but in a split second the words "No thanks" slipped out and deep regret replaced my longing. Before I knew it the weekend was over and my opportunity with it.

A point comes in every story when a decision must be made, a step taken, and a destination either pursued or abandoned to the silent ponderings of *"What if…?"* As anyone who has gotten stuck in the rut of fear knows, doing nothing *is* doing something. A prolonged pause is, for all intents and purposes, abandoning the pursuit. Sitting down at the wrong time can easily abort a journey and change the goal. *"Maybe next time…"* usually means *"Maybe never."*

Forward movement is essential for growth.

Being a disciple of Jesus is no exception. Jesus calls you to *follow* Him. To become like Him. To allow Him to live again on earth *through* you. This takes forward movement. Faith requires advancing motion. You might not know what you'll find or where you're going, but you must *choose* to take the next step if you want to continue the journey with Him. Only rarely do you fall forward by accident.

As with my waterskiing experience, all you need is in place: a lifejacket of grace is at hand to empower and uphold you; a mighty host surrounds and cheers you on; and the Holy Spirit is your Teacher leading to all truth. The only risk lies in saying, *"Maybe later..."*

While putting together this collection of meditations, the Holy Spirit prompted me with the title *Diving Boards and Trampolines*. I scribbled it down immediately, as it captures a higher purpose and essence of the book. Each reflection is an opportunity to explore, an excuse to try new ground, and a platform to launch you to new dimensions of relationship with Jesus and in life. The value of this book lies not only in the meditations, themselves, but where they will lead you.

Consider this: You would never set up camp on a diving board or build a house on a trampoline. They are not parking spaces, but launching pads, taking those who are willing to deeper depths and higher heights. Launching pads speak of possibility, adventure, and rewards.

In the same way, these pages are points of transition. They call for both thought *and* action.

Being a disciple of Christ demands you go forward yet more and more each day, into the glorious unfolding of your unity with the Trinity. This unfolding will not only reveal the majesty of your Maker, but your destiny and calling as His child, friend, servant, ambassador, priest, and bride.

You were created in Christ to search out hidden treasure and jump to higher ground. He calls you from faith to faith and glory to glory. Each new day holds the promise of a step forward. A step closer. A step deeper into the One who encompasses all you desire and hope for.

Russian author Fyodor Dostoyevsky may be accurate in his words, "Taking a new step, uttering a new word is what people fear the most." Going into the unknown can be very intimidating. Yet we were never meant to do this in our own strength and fortitude. Jesus sent us the perfect Guide and Helper, the Holy Spirit.

If you're like me, you may have this crazy idea that you're supposed to know how to do something *before* you do it. But Jesus has a very different perspective:

> *"I tell you the truth, anyone who doesn't receive the Kingdom of God like a child will never enter it"* (Luke 18:17, NLT).

I encourage you, come as a child. Come curious. Come expectant. Come with laughter and questions and the willingness to make mistakes along the way. Come and see and touch Him. Soon He'll capture your heart in new ways and you'll wonder why you waited so long to embrace such joy.

How to Read This Book

The reflections in this journal came in the movement of everyday life, while washing dishes and cooking dinner; driving to town or on a morning walk. They came in the flow of conversation with the Holy Spirit or as sweet interruptions to my day. They are meant to make one contemplate – and then create. To pause – and then pursue.

This pursuit will look different for each individual, yet carry a similar rhythm and fragrance. It's not about doing one specific activity or ritual, but building relationship – with your Creator, yourself, and those who surround your days.

Each meditation is followed by a blank page, ready for your input. Record scripture or journal observations; sketch thoughts or paste in pictures. There's no right or wrong way to use the space. However and whatever God choses to speak, pour it out upon these pages. Take the simple reflections I offer, pause, and then jump.

I chose to include a creative side to this journal as our God first introduces Himself as our Creator. And we, each one, are made in His image. Some of you may already express this trait in vast and varied ways. Others may not see yourself as having a creative nature at all – but you do! It's just waiting to be discovered.

I know because I have uncovered new dimensions of my creative side in the last year and I'll never turn back. How often we find what we've long desired in the very thing we avoid. We encounter the One who fills *all* with His glory – even us. What joy He brings to dry, dusty, dark corners. What color and light and beauty.

One note of caution: Getting to know God is not like a lap pool, but a vast, deep ocean and an endless mountain range.

- Take your time with each entry. (*Days, weeks, months, whatever it takes.*)
- Consider.
- Pray.
- Listen.
- Use other resources to expand your study.
- Worship with your pen, your pencils, your brush, your camera, your life.

We're on a journey of eternal proportions and the Author and Finisher of your faith longs for you to go deeper *in* Him and higher *with* Him.

- Permit truth to renew your mind.
- Expect new thoughts and ideas, new dreams and realities to take shape.
- Expect the fruit of God's Spirit to grow on you even as the Tree of Life.
- Step out and see His plans rise up to meet you.

The Kingdom of God is at hand, but only those who look for it will see. Only those who accept the invitation will taste. Only those who go beyond themselves will experience the destiny God has waiting.

Holy One, thank You for seeking me out; for inviting me in; for taking me on this journey. May anticipation rise up within to hear, to see, to know You even as I am known.

(1)
Don't despise small beginnings. God knows the perfect setting to encourage growth and emphasize beauty.

"The Lord will work out his plans for my life –
for your faithful love, O Lord, endures forever…"
Psalm 138:8, NLT

(2) I love when a new path – physical or spiritual – leads me to unexpected beauty. Explore one today and ask the Holy Spirit to show you what He sees.

(3)

May the fragrance of God's love capture you at every turn today!

"Your oils have a pleasing fragrance,
Your name is *like* purified oil..."
Song of Solomon 1:3, NASB

(4)
Some days, it's not so much about what you get done, but believing in all He's doing...

(5) Never get distracted into thinking the lock on your prison door is somehow unique or beautiful. *Freedom is beautiful!*

"So if the Son sets you free, you are truly free."
John 8:36, NLT

(6)
Today: Simplify.
What you have, what you do, what you focus on.
Allow what is valuable to rise to the top!

(7) Believing in your insecurities instead of what God says about you is like focusing on a broken padlock hanging from an open gate: It doesn't keep you from going through. It only intimidates you into not trying.

Step over the threshold.

(8)
    For just a moment,
    let the details draw you in.

Savor them.
Let them fill you with wonder.

His glory is hidden in these.

(9)

No amount of logic, reasoning, or planning can take you where the Holy Spirit wants to lead you. It's okay. Trust Him.

> "Teach me to do Your will,
> For You are my God;
> Let Your good Spirit lead me on level ground."
> Psalm 143:10, NASB

(10) You can't fully delight in your Creator until you realize how *fully* He delights in you. Come. Take a step closer to His smile…

(11)
Take time to linger today.
Time to think; to meditate.
From there you will hear, and live, more fully.

(12)

Holy Spirit, overwhelm me today. Flood in and water my soul with Your presence.

"He who believes in Me, as the Scripture said,
'From his innermost being will flow rivers of living water.'"
John 7:38, NASB

(13)

The Holy Spirit always speaks to your potential, your destiny. Even in discipline He points to who you truly are.

(14)

The safest, scariest, most wonderful place to be:
Over your head in Jesus!

What does that look like to you?

(15)
    The miracle of Christ in you:
        You don't *have* to be holy.
        You *get* to be holy.

"The Spirit Himself bears witness with our spirit that we are children of God."
Romans 8:16, NKJV

(16)

You may feel small, but if you carry the Light of Christ, it can guide countless ships to safety. Stand tall.

"You are the light of the world.
A town built on a hill cannot be hidden."
Matthew 5:14, NIV

(17)

Every so often, just sit down and let yourself be overwhelmed by the fact that you're a child of God.

(18)
Your Creator is incredibly persistent, incredibly patient. He's not intimidated by your weaknesses, but steadily leads you into your true identity.

Who does He say you are?

(19)

Sometimes the most profound beauty and wisdom are found in the most common things. Look again.

> "Four things on earth are small,
> yet they are extremely wise..."
> Proverbs 30:24, NIV

(20)

Intimacy with God necessitates obedience.

Where obedience is not a dominant force in your life reveals where your heart is still your own.

(21)
    Love never sets others up to fail without you.
    It builds them up to soar even higher than you do.

> "There is no greater love than to
> lay down one's life for one's friends."
> John 15:13, NLT

(22)

There's something so hopeful about a seed. It speaks of a future. A harvest. More than you now see.

Plant something today...

(23)
Today, this is my worship:
Holy oneness with You –
My God, my Creator,
My Comfort, my Friend.

(24)

Don't judge today by what you see.
Each step rings with eternity.

(25)

It's true: All roads don't lead to God. Yet He pursues you down whatever road you've wandered and draws you to Himself.

> "...Won't he leave the ninety-nine others in the wilderness and go to search for the one that is lost until he finds it?"
> Luke 15:4-5, NLT

(26)
Often, no words are needed.
Your heartbeat becomes your prayer, your praise.

(27)

Taking flight involves setting your gaze and lifting your wings. Go ahead. His plans are good.

(28)

When God made you in His image and breathed His Life into you, He made you capable of seeing beauty in the unadorned.

Ask for eyes to see...

(29)

Sometimes when you're focusing on the big issues, God wants you to see that He is also in the tiny details. He wants you to trust on a more intimate level.

"For forty years I led you through the wilderness,
yet your clothes and sandals did not wear out."
Deuteronomy 29:5, NLT

(30) Sometimes, we wish God would be obvious, to shout out what He want us to do. But He loves to draw near and whisper...

Listen.

(31)
What's keeping you from moving forward? Write it out and let God show you how small the obstacle is in His Kingdom.

(32)

Go to the Source.
Know why you believe what you believe.
Truth is worth it.

(33)
    Beauty is vast and deep and wide.
    Don't put a label or limits on it.
    Ask the Holy Spirit to see what eyes may miss.

*"Ears to hear and eyes to see —
both are gifts from the Lord."
Proverbs 20:12, NLT*

(34)
The Holy Spirit speaks in so many ways...
How is He speaking to you today?

Dreams.

Visions.

The Bible.

Friends.

Creation.

Audibly.

(35)
Thank You, Holy One, for so great a love as this: You never sleep but keep my soul even in the night hours.

(36)

Speak life over someone today and call them forth to be who their Creator sees them to be!

"A word fitly spoken is like
apples of gold in a setting of silver."
Proverbs 25:11, ESV

(37)
    Even when you're weary, He's not.
    And just sitting still with Him makes you not too.

(38)

The enemy of your soul has won just as surely when you fall into fear as when you sit in ignorance. Draw closer to Perfect Love who casts out fear.

(39)
Run with your feet, but rest with your heart.

"Look carefully then how you walk!
Live purposefully *and* worthily *and* accurately..."
Ephesians 5:15, AMP

(40)
Always answer lies with the truth – quickly. Never entertain ideas from one who wants to destroy you.

"The thief comes only to steal and kill and destroy.
I came that they may have life and have it abundantly."
John 10:10, ESV

(41)
Courage is not ignoring your fears, but sizing them up and declaring who God is in comparison.

(42)
Holy Spirit, be my filter.

"Give me your heart, my son,
And let your eyes delight in my ways."
Proverbs 23:26, NASB

(43)

The Eternal One doesn't want you to just acknowledge Him. He wants you to become wholly one with Him in Christ.

"...even as You, Father, *are* in Me and I in You,
that they also may be in Us..."
John 17:21, NASB

(44)

The core of endurance is *trust*.

Maintaining to the end isn't so much about action as it is about *rest*: Resting in truth; resting in hope; resting in the One who is your all.

(45)
Today, may I cut out clutter, leaving a place for You to be revealed. May I be simple so You can be profound.

(46)

Even when you don't know the way or the answer, know that He is both.

"Jesus answered,
'*I am* the way and the truth and the life.'"
John 14:6, NIV (emphasis mine)

(47)

Some treasures, some mysteries, can only be seen in deep places. Dive into the One who made the deep.

"Deep calls to deep at the sound of Your waterfalls;
All Your breakers and Your waves
have rolled over me."
Psalm 42:7, NASB

(48)

Don't let storm clouds frighten you. You're standing in a field of God's faithfulness. The coming rain carries promises of life.

Recount His faithfulness to you...

(49)

Stand up and declare who God is in the midst of your circumstances. Fill the atmosphere with truth and let darkness know you haven't forgotten: *It will never overcome the Light.*

(50)

Having the right tools does not a builder make.

Holy God, take my hand. Teach me, train me, lead me to my destiny in You.

What tool is the Holy Spirit training you to use today?

(51)

Although you may start out afraid that God sees and knows all, you will grow to treasure it! He is a Refuge of perfect rest.

*"...I sing for joy
in the shadow of your wings."*
Psalm 63:7, NLT

(52)

Holy Spirit, strengthen me today to do the thing I know I should, but keep pushing away.

(53)
An honest heart cries out in pain to the Father, but submits under the gentle surgery of His Spirit.[1]

(54)
Don't despise the process, for here you will learn the tender sound of your Savior's voice.

"My sheep listen to my voice;
I know them, and they follow me."
John 10:27, NLT

(55)

The Light of God is not meant to shame you, but to free you.

(56)

"The heavens hang low, full to overflowing –
Making it hard to breathe
Making it hard to see anything but You,
Anything but You – You're everywhere."[2]

(57)

Grace: Not just a word, but a force of love pouring forth day after day after day – even when you least expect or deserve it.

"May God give you more and more grace and peace as you grow in your knowledge of God and Jesus our Lord."
2 Peter 1:2, NLT

(58)

Today, in every step, every task, may I

- Gaze
- Behold
- Meditate
- Dwell with You…

(59)

> "O God, thou art my God; early will I seek thee..."
> Psalm 63:1, KJV

First thing, before desire turns to desperation, take time to listen.

> "In the morning, O Lord, You will hear my voice;
> In the morning I will order *my prayer* to You and *eagerly* watch."
> Psalm 5:3, NASB

(60)

Sometimes you're too close to get an accurate picture. Ask those you respect to help you see the bigger picture... We need each other.

(61)
You may feel like time is standing still, but it's not! God is moving. Change is happening.

What clues do you see of God's faithfulness?

(62)
If you never survey the horizon, you'll never ride the waves. Look up. Dream. Live.

(63) Start with *"I'm thankful for..."* and see how long you can go. There's so much when you look in the right direction.

> "Blessing and glory and wisdom and thanksgiving
> and honor and power and strength belong to our God
> forever and ever! Amen."
> Revelation 7:12, NLT

(64)

Today: Rise up in His resurrection Life! Rise up and dream and hope. Rise up, even as He has risen – and still rises each day to meet you.

(65)
We must never assume to know God's plans. Yet, you can know *Him* and completely trust the truth of His love, power, and wisdom. All His ways lead to Life.

(66)
Only God truly understands the full extent of His love for you... but He delights in unfolding it piece by piece.

(67)
God's purpose is not to frighten you. He has no desire to intimidate or manipulate. But if you never come to see the vast expanse between Him as the Creator and you as the created, you risk being encumbered by either pride or apathy. Godly fear opens your eyes to the power of God. It sets you on a pathway of trust.

(68)
Fill your mind with truth and your heart will overflow from its abundance.

"O Lord God, You are God, and Your words are truth,
and You have promised this good thing to Your servant."
2 Samuel 7:28, NASB

(69)
You were never meant to figure life out on your own. God created you with *relationship* in mind.

(70)

When you worry about what others think or say about you, you miss what God's saying. His words trump all others.

"The Lord merely spoke, and the heavens were created.
He breathed the word, and all the stars were born."
Psalm 33:6, NLT

(71)

Always let your joy lead you back to Jesus. All pleasure should find its roots in heaven.

"I have told you this so that My joy may be in you
and that your joy may be complete."
John 15:11, NIV

(72)

Are you pushing God along, thinking you're missing an opportunity? In His mercy, He's waiting, building, and fashioning you; training you to be ready... so you won't be in the right place at the wrong time.

Rejoice in today. Enjoy it.
It is preparing you for tomorrow.

(73)

When you seek, you will find. If you find yourself in a place you don't want to be, reevaluate what you're seeking.

(74)

What greater peace could you have than in the One who created it all, knows it all, holds it all, and is motivated in all things by an eternal passion for you?

Sketch what this looks like to you.

(75)

God longs to give you His perspective – for you to see through His eyes, His heart, His wisdom, and power. But for that, you must be intimately close to Him. *Draw me nearer, Father.*

> "But as for me, how good it is to be near God!"
> Psalm 73:28a, NLT

(76)
When you think you can't hold on, let your Creator-God hold you. The next step leads to freedom and joy.

(77)
How sweet the friendship of one who walks in humility and grace. *May I be such a friend.*

(78)

Jehovah makes everything beautiful in its time. For every season He is perfect.

What is blooming in your life today?

(79)

When you have no other place to go, you come to realize the One you needed was there all along.

> "But Simon Peter answered Him,
> 'Lord, to whom shall we go?
> You have the words of eternal life.'"
> John 6:68, NKJV

(80)
Expect to hear the Holy Spirit speak and watch Him turn up the volume. He loves for you to hear Him!

(81)

Some things cannot be fully enjoyed in passing.
You have to sit down in the middle of it.

Go ahead – do it.

(82)

Ever wonder what Jesus and the Spirit are praying for you? Be still. Listen. It's worth agreeing with.

Romans 8:27

Romans 8:34

(83)

Once you glimpse, as through a keyhole, even a small portion of what God is doing – every second, every breath, every hour – you will never again pray for Him to move, but only to be able to see, agree, and be a part of His vast plan.

> "How great are His signs and how mighty are His wonders!
> His kingdom is an everlasting kingdom
> And His dominion is from generation to generation."
> Daniel 4:3, NASB

(84)
There's a big difference between walking the narrow path with Jesus and being in a rut. If you're bored, make sure you're still walking together. He is never boring!

(85)
Take time to make music today – with or without an instrument. The earth needs your sound.

(86)

Just because you're in *this* season doesn't mean you can't dream about the next one.

Imagine for a moment what you want it to look like...

(87)
Today, take time out just to appreciate the rhythm of your breathing. Life is so much more than being busy.

"This is what the Sovereign Lord says: Look! I am going to put breath into you and make you live again!"
Ezekiel 37:5, NLT

(88)

The Holy Spirit always gets to the heart of an issue... Let Him. He loves to bring hope and freedom!

"It was for freedom that Christ set us free;
therefore keep standing firm and
do not be subject again to a yoke of slavery."
Galatians 5:1, NASB

Endnotes

1 Litzelman, Amy Layne. 2010. *This Beloved Road: A Journey of Revelation and Worship*. Oklahoma City, OK: Tate Publishing. 173.
2 Litzelman, Amy Layne. *Faith's Reality*.

Other books by Amy Layne Litzelman

This Beloved Road – A Journey of Revelation and Worship

This Beloved Road Workbook

This Beloved Road Vol. II – Into the Source

Diving Boards & Trampolines Vol. II

A Worshiper's Manifesto

www.ingramcontent.com/pod-product-compliance
Lightning Source LLC
Chambersburg PA
CBHW071724040426
42446CB00011B/2211